D1418590

POSTMAN PAT

CAN YOU SPOT?

POLICE

PAT 4

igloobooks

PAT'S BUSY DAY

Welcome to Greendale. Postman Pat and Jess are ready for another busy day making their deliveries. Why don't you join them and see what exciting things you can find on the way? Search for Pat and Jess in each scene of this fun book, then try to find the other hidden objects and characters, too.

Postman Pat **Jess** **Sara Clifton** **Julian Clifton** **Ajay Bains**

Mrs Goggins **Bonnie** **Alf Thompson** **Ted Glen** **Ben Taylor** **Michael Lam**

Look at the characters on this page. Now try to find them in the scene opposite. Can you spot them all? Then, see if you can find the other hidden items.

3 ✓

5 ✓

7 ✓

When you've found these items, you're ready to start!

COUNTRY CHAOS

Oh dear. Look at all the animals blocking the road! It's going to take a very long time to get past them all. Can you spot Pat and Jess? Can you find Alf in this busy country scene, too?

PAT 4

1

3

6

6

8

10

SPECIAL DELIVERIES

There are lots of letters and parcels at the Sorting Office for Pat to deliver today. Where is Ben hiding? Can you find Pat and Jess quickly so they can get straight to work?

1

3

5

6

8

10

ALL ABOARD

Pat and Jess have dropped Julian off at the station so he can catch the train to the seaside with his friends. Can you see Pat, Jess and Julian? Look up high to find Jess!

Now can you find
all of these items?

1

4

5

6

8

10

TIME FOR TEA

Look at all the yummy cakes in the cafe! Pat and Jess have popped by to see Sara. Can you find Michael hiding, too?

1

4

4

6

10

12

PENCASTER SQUARE

There's a lot going on in Pencaster today. Pat's parked his bike in the Square but can't remember where! Can you help him find it? Don't forget to find Pat and Jess, too.

Now can you spot these?

1

4

4

6

8

15

FIX IT UP

Uh-oh. Pat's van needs a quick repair so they've taken it to the garage. Pat and Jess are waiting for the van to be fixed, where are they? Can you see Ted working hard?

Now look for
these items, too.

1

4

3

4

6

8

PAT 4

PAT'S PARCELS

Can you see Pat and Jess at the Sorting Office? Where is
Ben hiding? Can you spot the SDS helicopter, too?

Can you see all these things, too?

1

5

4

7

8

10

FLYING HIGH

Where are Pat and Jess this time? Try looking up to the sky to find them. When you've found them, look for Ted and his next customer at the garage, PC Selby.

Can you find these things, too?

1

2

4

8

8

10

TICKETS PLEASE

Ajay is busy making sure the trains leave the station on time.
Can you see him waving? Now, where are Pat and Jess?

PENCASTER

Look for these items, too.

1

4

4

6

8

10

FABULOUS FRIENDS

What a busy day. Now it's time for Pat and Jess to go home for a rest. Can you see them? Nine of Pat's friends have come to say goodbye, too. Can you see them all?

Look for these items, too.

1

2

4

6

8

10

WELL DONE!

You've found everything, but how closely were you paying attention?
All ten of the items below are hidden in each scene. Can you find them all, too?

BONUS FIND

A special Golden
Stamp is also hiding
in one of the scenes.
Go back through
the book and see
if you can find it.

Golden Stamp

WELL DONE!
MISSION ACCOMPLISHED!